Helping Children See Jesus

ISBN: 978-1-64104-039-6

SATAN
The Enemy of God
New Testament Volume 2: Life of Christ Part 2

Author: Ruth B. Greiner
Illustrator: Frances H. Hertzler
Computer Graphic Artists: Joshua Day, Yuko Willoughby
Typesetting and Layout: Morgan Melton, Patricia Pope

© 2018 Bible Visuals International
PO Box 153, Akron, PA 17501-0153
Phone: (717) 859-1131
www.biblevisuals.org

All rights reserved. No part of this publication may be reproduced, stored in a retrieval system or transmitted in any form by any means, electronic, mechanical, photocopy, recording or otherwise, without the prior permission of the publisher, except as provided by USA copyright law.

RELATED ITEMS

To access related items (such as activities, memory verse posters and translated texts) please visit our web store at www.biblevisuals.org and enter 1002 at the top right of the web page. You may need to reduce the zoom setting to get the search box.

FREE TEXT DOWNLOAD

To obtain a FREE printable copy of the English teaching text (PDF format) under Product Format, please scroll down and select Extra–PDF Teacher Text Download. Then under Language select English before clicking the ADD TO CART button to place in your shopping cart. Other languages are available at an additional cost from the Language menu. When checking out, use coupon code XTACSV17 at checkout and click on Apply Coupon to receive the discount on the English text.

Know your Saviour

1 John 4:4, 9; Luke 2:41; John 10:29–30; Romans 5:28; John 14:6; Luke 2:52; John 1:12; 1 John 5:4; Galatians 1:4

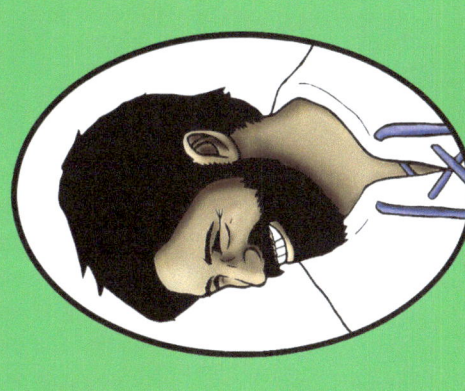

Know about your enemy

2 Corinthians 2:11; Romans 16:20; Matthew 8:33; Revelation 12:9; 2 Corinthians 11:13–15; John 8:44; Ephesians 6:11; 2 Corinthians 4:4; 1 Peter 5:8

Know how to use your sword

2 Timothy 3:15-17; Ephesians 6:17; Hebrews 4:12; Psalm 119:11; Mark 3:31

© Bible Visuals International Inc

Ye are of God, little children, and have overcome them: because **Greater is He that is in you,** than he that is in the world. 1 John 4:4

Lesson 1
THE ENEMY OF THE NEW KING

Scripture to be studied: Matthew 2:12-23; Luke 2:39-52

The *aim* of the lesson: To show that God is greater than Satan.

What your students should *know*: Because they do not always do right, they need to turn to God for help to overcome Satan.

What your students should *feel*: A desire to be obedient in all things as Jesus was.

What your students should *do*: Ask God to help them to be obedient.

Lesson outline (for the teacher's and students' notebooks):

1. Satan tries to kill God's Son (Matthew 2:12, 16-18).
2. God protects His Son (Matthew 2:13-15, 19-23).
3. Teachers are amazed at Jesus' wisdom (Luke 2:39-49).
4. Jesus obeyed God and his parents (Luke 2:50-52).

NOTE TO THE TEACHER

In our last volume, we learned of the coming of God to earth in the form of man. The birth of the Lord Jesus Christ–and all of the events connected with it–testify that He is indeed the Son of God.

In this volume, we learn how Satan, the enemy of God, does all that he can to get rid of the Lord Jesus. Satan has always opposed the will of God. He always will oppose the will of God. Ever since the awful day in eternities past when Satan said, "I will be like the Most High God" (Isaiah 14:14), he has sought to prove that he is superior to God. But the verse of Scripture that we are going to be memorizing during these lessons is true:

Ye are of God, little children, and have overcome them: because greater is He that is in you, than he that is in the world. (1 John 4:4)

THE LESSON

You will remember that in our last lesson we learned that God had told the Wise Men (in a dream) that they were not to return to Jerusalem. So they went home another way. But Herod the king was waiting for the Wise Men to come back to tell him where Christ had been born.

Because of this, all was not well in the palace. King Herod paced the floor. You can imagine how angry he was. "Where are they?" he doubtless shouted. "They should have been back long before this. I commanded those men from the East to come and tell me when they found the Child–that newborn king. How dare they disobey me?"

1. SATAN TRIES TO KILL GOD'S SON
Matthew 2:12, 16-18

When Herod learned that the Wise Men had returned to their own land without coming back through Jerusalem, he was furious. "They have tricked me! They have tricked me!" he roared.

Show Illustration #1

Quickly he wrote an order for his soldiers: "Go kill all the baby boys two years old and younger in and around Bethlehem."

Pushing the order into the hands of the captain, he shouted, "We'll see about this new King of the Jews. I'll get rid of Him. There will be no other king. I am the king–Herod the Great. No one will take my place."

Immediately the soldiers marched to Bethlehem. From house to house they went, destroying every baby boy who was two years old or less, exactly as Herod had commanded. Mothers sobbed and pleaded. Fathers wept. Children tried to hide. But the soldiers went to each house obeying the horrible command of wicked King Herod.

Herod was proud of his plan. But let me tell you something that Herod did not know. He was really carrying out the plan of a more powerful enemy of God. That enemy is Satan. Once Satan had been a beautiful angel guarding the presence of God. But he had become proud and wanted to be greater than God. Since pride is sin, and sin must be punished, God punished Satan by taking away from him the high position that had been his. Ever since then Satan has tried to get men and women and boys and girls to obey him rather than God.

King Herod was pleased when he learned that his order had been obeyed. "Now all the baby boys in Bethlehem are dead!" he exclaimed. "The new king is dead."

2. GOD PROTECTS HIS SON
Matthew 2:13-15, 19-23

But God, who knows everything, had known of the plan of Herod. Right after the Wise Men had visited Jesus, an angel from God had appeared to Joseph in a dream. "Get up," the angel whispered. "Take the Child and His mother and go to Egypt. Stay there until I tell you to leave. Herod will be looking for the Child to kill Him."

Show Illustration #2

So while others slept, Joseph and Mary had packed quickly and left Bethlehem. Tenderly they protected the Son of God through the dark night. The message of the angel must have gone over and over in their minds: "Herod will be looking for the Child to kill Him." But they remembered also the other words of the angel: "Go to Egypt. Stay there until I tell you to leave." *We will get to Egypt,* they thought. *God is greater than Herod. God is greater than Satan, the master of Herod. God will keep us safe.*

God did keep them safe as they hurried to Egypt. He was working out His plan, even though Satan was trying to destroy it.

(*Teacher:* Keep illustrations out of sight from now until it is time to show #3.)

Later, King Herod died. Then an angel spoke to Joseph in a dream, saying, "Get up. Take the Child and His mother and go back to the country of Israel. Those who tried to kill the Child are dead." Again Joseph obeyed God. With Mary and Jesus he went back to Nazareth, the village in which they lived before Jesus was born.

In Nazareth, Jesus grew as any boy does. But He was different in one way–He was *always* good. He never said a wrong word. He was always obedient. He was never mean or selfish. He never went to a wrong place. He never had one wrong thought!

Satan, the enemy of God, must have tried many times to make Jesus do wrong. But Jesus did not sin. (See Hebrews 4:15.) Never once did the Lord Jesus do one wrong thing. He was perfect always!

3. TEACHERS ARE AMAZED AT JESUS' WISDOM
Luke 2:39-49

By the time Jesus reached the age of 12, He was strong and wise; and God, His Father, was well pleased with Him. Now He was old enough to go to the Passover Feast just as all other Jewish boys His age. Jesus had heard many things about the Passover, that wonderful and exciting feast in the Temple. Crowds of people went to Jerusalem from all parts of the land once every year for this feast.

Mary and Joseph packed for the journey. Then together with many of their friends, they traveled to Jerusalem for the big event. We do not know how many days the trip took, but at last they saw Jerusalem, the capital of Palestine. Most wonderful of all, they saw the magnificent Temple, the House of God! If only the people who were there had known that He, Jesus, was the Son of God, they would have bowed down and worshiped Him. But they did not know.

The Temple was beautiful. The people gazed at the gold and silver gate, the marble steps, the large pillars, the altar of sacrifice and the golden candlesticks. Jesus knew that this was His Father's House.

There was singing in the Temple and the sound of silver trumpets. Sacrifices were made by the priests. The Scriptures were read by the teachers of the Law of God. At last the celebration was all over for another year.

People began their journey home. As Joseph and Mary walked with their friends, they talked of the wonderful things they had heard and seen. On and on they went.

It was almost the end of the first day of their journey when Mary realized she had not seen Jesus along the road. He was not with Joseph or the other men. He was not with the boys his age. She could not find Him anywhere.

Sadly Mary and Joseph hurried back to Jerusalem. Where could He be? Reaching the city, they went from one place to another asking, "Have you seen Jesus?" But always the answer was, "No, we have not seen Him."

Three days they hunted for Him. Then they thought of the Temple. *Can He be there?* they wondered.

Through the large gates, up the steps and into the Temple they hurried.

Show Illustration #3

There He was! He was sitting with great and wise teachers–teachers of the Law of God. Jesus, who was only twelve years old, was talking with those educated men. And they were amazed at His understanding and answers!

Mary and Joseph rushed to Jesus. "Why have You done this to us?" Mary asked. "We have been searching everywhere for You. We have been worried and sad."

"But why did you need to search for Me?" Jesus asked. "Did you not know that I would be here in the House of my Father?"

4. JESUS OBEYED GOD AND HIS PARENTS
Luke 2:50-52

Joseph and Mary did not really understand what Jesus meant. But they were eager to be on their way. So Jesus, the Son of God, rose immediately and went with them out of the Temple and back to their home in Nazareth.

Show Illustration #4

There at home Jesus obeyed Mary and Joseph always. Each day He helped Joseph with his work in the carpenter shop. In every way He did exactly what His heavenly Father wanted Him to do. So Jesus grew both tall and wise and was loved by God and man.

There was one who never, never loved Him. That was His enemy, Satan. We have seen in the early part of this lesson how Satan tried to kill the Lord Jesus when He was a baby. You will not want to miss the next class, when we shall see how Satan again tried to get rid of the Lord Jesus when He was a Man. But remember always that the Father God and God the Son can never be defeated . . . never!

(You, teacher, will know the needs of your students. They understand that they are quite unlike the Son of God. They do not always do what is right. [Nor do we teachers always do right!] Satan is powerful. But our students and we can turn to God for help to overcome the enemy of God, Satan. Let us pray that we, like the Lord Jesus, shall be obedient in all matters. And may we enjoy victory in our Christian lives, by the help of God.)

Lesson 2
THE BAPTISM OF THE LORD JESUS AND HIS TEMPTATION

Scripture to be studied: Matthew 3:1-17; 4:1-11; Mark 1:1-13; Luke 3:1-18; John 1:6-8; 1:15-34

The *aim* of the lesson: To show that the Lord Jesus always did what His Father wanted Him to do.

What your students should *know*: Jesus overcame Satan by memorizing and quoting the Word of God.

What your students should *feel*: Incapable of doing right in their own strength.

What your students shou*ld do*: Memorize Scripture and trust God to help them overcome their temptations.

Lesson outline (for the teacher's and students' notebooks):
1. God declares that Christ is His Son (Matthew 3:1-17; Mark 1:1-11; Luke 3:1-18; John 1:6-8, 15-34).
2. Christ refuses to disobey His Father (Matthew 4:1-4; Mark 1:12-13).
3. Jesus refuses to show His greatness (Matthew 4:5-7).
4. Jesus refuses to worship Satan (Matthew 4:8-11).

The verse to be memorized:
Ye are of God, little children, and have overcome them: because greater is He that is in you, than he that is in the world. (1 John 4:4)

NOTE TO THE TEACHER
This is a lesson that should be helpful to those who are already members of the family of God. The one weapon that the Lord Jesus used against Satan was the Word of God. As we learn God's Word and obey it, it will help us, also, to be victorious over Satan and sin.

You will have much to study from the Word of God when you prepare this lesson. All of the Gospels tell us the events. So read carefully, read prayerfully.

THE LESSON

Do you remember our last lesson? What was it about? (*Teacher:* Help your pupils by asking many questions. A few are suggested here.)

1. How did Satan try to get rid of the Son of God when He was a baby? (*Satan made Herod so jealous that he tried to kill the newborn king that the Wise Men told him about.*)
2. Where did Mary and Joseph find Jesus when he was missing? What was He doing? (*He was with the wise teachers in the Temple in Jerusalem.*)
3. What kind of life did the Lord Jesus live in His home? (*He obeyed Mary and Joseph always.*)
4. Was the Lord Jesus ever tempted to do wrong? (*Yes, He was tempted but did not sin.*)

We know very little about the Lord Jesus from the time He was 12 until He was a grown man, except that He worked as a carpenter's apprentice. From the time He was 30 years old until His death and resurrection, we know (from the Bible!) a great deal. In our lesson today we learn of another effort of Satan to get rid of the Lord Jesus.

Crowds of people were going to the desert. It was usually a lonely place. But on this particular day, people–many of them–left their homes in Jerusalem and the surrounding villages of Judea to go to the desert near the Jordan River. Why were they going? They were going to see a man–a strange man who wore a leather belt and clothes made from the hair of camels. This man had been living alone in the desert for some time. His food was locusts and wild honey.

Now he was no longer alone. People were coming from everywhere to hear him. They heard him cry out his message–a message that had been given to him by God: "Change your ways and be baptized and God will forgive your sins. Turn from sin to doing right for the Kingdom of Heaven is near, and the King is soon to come."

The people listened eagerly. They were curious. *Who is this man?* they wondered. Is he the Christ that is to come? Could this be the One of whom the prophets had written? No! The man in the desert was not the Christ–the Promised One from God. He was John the Baptist.

As the people gathered around the strange preacher, he called out to them: "I baptize you with water, but One who is much greater than I is coming. He is so high above me that I am not good enough to untie the strings of His sandals."

Many who heard John were sorry for their sins and decided to change their sinful ways. They desired to serve the true God and obey Him, even as John the Baptist was doing. So they asked John to baptize them in the Jordan River, as a sign that they had turned from their sins.

1. GOD DECLARES THAT CHRIST IS HIS SON
Matthew 3:1-17; Mark 1:1-11; Luke 3:1-18; John 1:6-8, 15-34

One day a Stranger joined the crowd that had gathered in the desert. He had come from Nazareth and now stood listening to John as he told the people to turn from their sins. The Stranger walked toward John. It was Jesus–the Christ–the very One of whom John had been preaching.

"I have come to be baptized," Jesus said.

"Surely you do not come to me to be baptized," John said. "Rather, I need *You* to baptize *me*!"

"It must be this way," Jesus said. "This is what God wants."

Show Illustration #5

So John agreed to baptize the Lord Jesus. But it was different from any other baptism John had seen. As the Lord Jesus came up out of the water, suddenly the heavens opened. And John saw the Spirit of God come down in the form of a dove and rest upon the Lord Jesus.

Then John heard a voice say, "This is My own dear Son. I am very pleased with Him." The voice had come from Heaven. It was the voice of God the Father. John realized immediately that he had just baptized God the Son. And God the Holy Spirit had come down upon Him. God–the three-in-one–was there at the Jordan River. John knew this was a definite sign from God to show that the Lord Jesus is indeed the Christ, the Son of God. He is the One of whom the prophets had written long before. He is the One for whom the people had long waited.

Why was God the Father pleased with His Son? Because He had come to earth and was obeying the Father in Heaven.

2. CHRIST REFUSES TO DISOBEY HIS FATHER
Matthew 4:1-4; Mark 1:12-13

But Satan was not pleased. He did not like it that Jesus had lived on earth for 30 years without doing anything wrong. He did not want Jesus to do the will of God the Father. And he was determined to make Jesus sin.

After the baptism of Jesus, Satan watched. He would wait for the right moment. He must have been glad when Jesus went alone into a desert. There were only wild animals there! But God the Father was watching over His Son.

Show Illustration #6

One day passed. Then two. The Lord Jesus had no food. How hungry He must have become!

Satan thought, *Jesus is hungry. Now I shall be able to get Him to obey me.*

To Jesus Satan said, "If You are the Son of God, tell these stones to turn into bread." He pointed at the hard, rough stones that lay scattered across the desert.

The Lord Jesus had power to do anything He wanted to do. He had created the world and everything in it. (See John 1:3; Colossians 1:16; Hebrews 1:10.) It would be easy for Him to change stones into bread. But He would not obey Satan. So He answered, "The Word of God says that bread will not feed the soul of man. Obedience to every word of God is what we need."

It did not matter to Jesus how hungry He was. The most important thing to Him was to obey God the Father always. If He would have done what Satan had said, He would have disobeyed His Father.

Satan had failed. But he was not ready to give up.

3. JESUS REFUSES TO SHOW HIS GREATNESS
Matthew 4:5-7

Show Illustration #7

Satan said to Jesus, "If You are the Son of God, throw Yourself down from the top of the Temple wall." (The Jews called the top of the Temple wall *the pinnacle* of the Temple.) Satan continued, "The Word of God says, 'God will send His angels to keep You from harm.' It also says, 'They will hold You up with their hands so You will not even hurt Your feet on the stones.'"

The Lord Jesus answered, "But the Word of God also says, 'Do not put the Lord God to a foolish test.'"

Christ Jesus had done that which was right. Satan was again defeated. But he did not give up.

4. JESUS REFUSES TO WORSHIP SATAN
Matthew 4:8-11

Show Illustration #8

This time Satan took Jesus to a very high mountain. There he showed the Son of God all the kingdoms of the world and their beauty. He showed Him the wealth, the power and the greatness of all the lands. "I will give all this to You if You will only kneel down and worship me," Satan said.

Kneel down and worship Satan and get all the countries of the world? Would it be worth it?

"Go away, Satan!" Jesus commanded. "The Word of God says: 'Worship only the Lord God and obey only Him.'"

Satan had lost again. This time, in obedience to the Son of God, he went away. Jesus had proved that He was stronger than His enemy, Satan. In all things Jesus obeyed God, His Father.

After Satan had gone, angels came and took care of Jesus. What a wonderful comfort that must have been to the Lord Jesus after those 40 long, hard days of temptation in the desert.

Jesus had been tempted by Satan to do wrong. But He did no wrong. Today, Satan tries to get us who belong to God to sin and disobey God. In our own strength we cannot resist him. But if we use the Word of God as the Lord Jesus did, we will be able to stand against Satan and obey God.

Are you studying the Word of God? Are you memorizing it? The Psalmist tells us, "Thy Word have I hid in mine heart, that I might not sin against Thee" (Psalm 119:11). Only as we learn the Word of God can we defeat Satan. A good verse to remember is 1 John 4:4. Say over and over again the end of that verse: "Greater is He [God] that is in you, than he [Satan] that is in the world." God *IS* greater than Satan. And if you are a child of God, the Spirit of God is living in your heart. As you ask Him to, He will help you to be victorious over every temptation of Satan.

(Now, teacher, remember that you must meet the needs of your students. As you visit them in their homes, you will see how this lesson can help them in their everyday living. Encourage them to memorize the Word of God. The Lord Jesus knew Scripture. That is why He could quote it to Satan. You will have to explain that we cannot do right in our own strength. We must ask God for His help and trust Him for it. Then we can be victorious over Satan.)

PRAYER FOR THE TEACHER

As you prepare this lesson and as you teach it, you will want to make this your prayer: "Dear Father in Heaven, help me to make clear the great truth of this lesson. Help me to speak with such conviction, and let the verses from the Bible be so clear, that each one I teach will realize that the Lord Jesus Christ is truly the Son of God. Help me to show my students how they can have the assurance of eternal life. May each one have the joy of sins forgiven."

Remember, Teacher: The Lord Jesus is praying for you!

Lesson 3
JESUS IN NAZARETH

Scripture to be studied: Luke 4:14-30

The *aim* of the lesson: To show that Jesus Christ allowed the power of God to control His life.

What your students should *know*: If they will receive the Lord Jesus Christ as Saviour, He will give them power to do that which pleases Him.

What your students should *feel*: A desire to let Jesus Christ control their lives.

What your students should *do*: Believe in Jesus as the Son of God and receive Him as Saviour from sin.

Lesson outline (for the teacher's and students' notebooks):
1. Jesus reads the Old Testament (Luke 4:14-19).
2. Jesus fulfills the Scriptures (Luke 4:20-21).
3. People reject the Son of God (Luke 4:22-28).
4. Satan tries to destroy Jesus (Luke 4:29-30).

The verse to be memorized:

Ye are of God, little children, and have overcome them: because greater is He that is in you, than he that is in the world. (1 John 4:4)

NOTE TO THE TEACHER

This is a section of the Word of God that is often overlooked. But it is equally important, you may be certain. Like the first two lessons in this volume, this is a record of another attempt of Satan to get rid of the Lord Jesus. Satan often uses a person or people to do his work. Once he used King Herod, you remember. In this lesson Satan uses people in Jesus' hometown, causing them to try to get rid of the Son of God. Let us never forget that Satan is powerful, but God is all-powerful!

As you study Luke 4:14-30 in the Bible, you will be amazed to see the power of God at work. Read the entire section many times. At the conclusion of your study, the truth of the verse that goes with these lessons, 1 John 4:4, will be sealed in your heart.

REVIEW

We have had two lessons proving that Satan tried to get rid of the Lord Jesus.

1. When did Satan make his first attempt to get rid of Jesus? *(At His birth)*
2. When the Lord Jesus was a grown man, what did Satan want Him to do? *(Satan wanted Jesus to obey him.)*
3. If Jesus had obeyed Satan, could we worship Him today as the Son of God? *(No, indeed!)*
4. Each time when He was tempted by Satan, the Lord Jesus said something important to Satan. From what scroll did Jesus get the words which He spoke? *(The Word of God)*
5. If we hide the Word of God in our hearts, what will it help us to do? *(Keep us from sinning; Psalm 119:11.)*

THE LESSON

Even though the Lord Jesus was a grown man (age 30), He had never once done one wrong thing. Satan had tried many times to cause the Son of God to sin. He had tried to get rid of the Lord Jesus. After so many attempts, do you think Satan gave up? Indeed he did not! Let us see in the lesson today what he tried to do.

The people who lived in Nazareth had heard strange things about a Man who had grown up in their city. They had learned that Jesus, who used to live in Nazareth, had mighty powers. He could do things that no ordinary man could do. He could heal sick people in a moment, make the blind see and the deaf hear and the crippled walk. Should they believe these stories? Could one who had been an ordinary carpenter in Nazareth now be a great teacher and prophet, as many people called Him? They did not know. If only they could see Him again and watch Him do one of His great miracles . . . if they could see His power for themselves, maybe *then* they would believe.

1. JESUS READS THE OLD TESTAMENT
Luke 4:14-19

Show Illustration #9

One day Jesus returned to His hometown of Nazareth. There, on the Sabbath Day, as usual, He went to the synagogue (the place where Jewish people went to worship God). It was the custom in the synagogue that when a person read the Word of God he stood up. Then he sat down to speak! So Jesus stood to read the Scriptures. The scroll of Isaiah the prophet was handed to Him. He opened the scroll and began to read: "It is written, 'The Spirit of the Lord is upon Me. He has anointed Me to preach the Good News to the poor; He has sent Me to announce that prisoners shall be set free, that the blind shall see, that the downtrodden shall be freed and to announce that God is ready to give blessings to all who come to Him' " (Isaiah 61:1).

2. JESUS FULFILLS THE SCRIPTURES
Luke 4:20-21

Show Illustration #10

Christ returned the Word of God to the attendant. Then He sat down. Everyone in the synagogue gazed at Him.

Jesus said, "Today this Scripture has come true."

The people were amazed! He was saying that what the Prophet Isaiah had foretold hundreds of years earlier had come true. Isaiah had said that Someone would come and preach the Good News to the poor, He would teach, He would heal the blind and He would set people free from their sins. Jesus was saying to the people in Nazareth that He was the One of whom Isaiah had spoken!

3. PEOPLE REJECT THE SON OF GOD
Luke 4:22-28

The people probably whispered among themselves, "Is not this the son of Joseph?" They could not believe that this One–

the carpenter–who used to live in their town, could possibly be the One of whom Isaiah had written. They would not believe in their hearts that He was the Son of God.

Jesus knew exactly what they were thinking. So He said, "I expect you will say, 'Why do You not do miracles here in Your hometown as You did in the city of Capernaum?' I tell you that no prophet is accepted in his own hometown."

Then the Lord Jesus told them of prophets of whom they knew (Elijah and Elisha). He reminded them that those great men had done miracles to help other people. But they had not helped their own people, probably because the people had not believed that these men were sent from God.

The people became angry. They wanted to see the Lord Jesus do miracles. If, as the Scriptures said, He was the One who would make blind people see, they wanted Him to do that kind of miracle at once.

Show Illustration #11

Because the Lord Jesus did not do a miracle, the people became furious. They made Him get out of the synagogue. They pushed Him down the street. They would get rid of Him!

4. SATAN TRIES TO DESTROY JESUS
Luke 4:29-30

Show Illustration #12

They led Jesus to the top of the hill. They would throw Him over the edge of the cliff and be rid of Him forever!

Then a strange thing happened. Jesus disappeared right through the crowd. Nobody could stop Him. It was a miracle! It was by the power of God.

Jesus went away from Nazareth–away from the people among whom He had once lived. Jesus went away because the people did not want Him. He did not do any miracles because they did not believe in Him as the Son of God. (See Mark 6:6; also Matthew 13:58.) Jesus had come to this world He had created but His own people would not receive Him. (See John 1:11.) They should have remembered what a perfect life He had lived as a boy. They should have known that anyone who preached as He did must have been from God.

Someone else was unhappy when Jesus was in Nazareth. He–Satan–had tried many times before to do away with the Son of God. He did not want the people of Nazareth to listen to Jesus. He did not want them to believe in Jesus. So he caused them to turn against Jesus. Seeing the people leading Jesus to the edge of the cliff, Satan thought he had been successful. But the power of God is far greater than the power of Satan.

The people in Nazareth did not turn to God for power. Rather they let the power of Satan turn them against the Saviour of the world. How sad!

Whose power is controlling *your* life? . . . the power of God or the power of Satan? If you receive the Lord Jesus Christ as Saviour, He will give you His power–the power of God–to control your life and to cause you to do the things that please Him.

(*Teacher:* Have you determined what should be your purpose in teaching this lesson to your group? Clearly, the Lord Jesus allowed the power of God to control His life. God is willing to control our lives, if we let Him. But He gives His power only to those who belong to Him through faith in Christ the Lord. Encourage your students to place their trust in the Son of God and receive Him as Saviour from sin.)

Lesson 4
SATAN

Scripture to be studied: Ezekiel 28:11-19; Isaiah 14:12-15
The *aim* of the lesson: To show who Satan really is.

What your students should *know*: Satan tries to keep people from receiving the Lord Jesus and tries to cause believers to do wrong. Only through God can they overcome Satan.

What your students should *feel*: The need to know Jesus Christ and rely on Him.

What your students should *do*:
Unsaved: Believe on Jesus as the Son of God and receive Him as Saviour from sin.
Saved: Listen and obey God, confess all sin.

Lesson outline (for the teacher's and students' notebooks):
1. Lucifer, the angel of light, becomes Satan (Ezekiel 28:11-19; Isaiah 14:12-15).
2. Adam and Eve, controlled by Satan, sin (Genesis 3:1-24).
3. Christ dies for sinners (Genesis 3:15).
4. Satan defeated (Revelation 20:10).

The verse to be memorized:
Ye are of God, little children, and have overcome them: because greater is He that is in you, than he that is in the world. (1 John 4:4)

NOTE TO THE TEACHER

We have had three lessons showing how Satan, the enemy of God, tried to get rid of the Son of God. Today we want to review those lessons simply. Then we shall study a few more facts about Satan. In future studies we shall learn more about him.

By now, you and your students should have 1 John 4:4 memorized perfectly.

THE LESSON

1. LUCIFER, THE ANGEL OF LIGHT, BECOMES SATAN
Ezekiel 28:11-19; Isaiah 14:12-15

Show Illustration #13

Lucifer, Son of the Morning, was the anointed (chosen) angel of God. His home was in Heaven. He had been created by God long before Adam and Eve lived upon the earth. Lucifer was more beautiful than anything we can imagine. His clothing was trimmed with precious stones: diamonds, rubies, emeralds and many others, all set in fine gold. How brilliant and colorful he must have been! The Bible says he was perfect in beauty and full of wisdom. Lucifer lived in the presence of God. There he did what God told him to do.

This beautiful angel had been chosen by God to rule in a very high place above other angels. The Word of God says he was perfect in every way. He thought no wrong. He did no wrong. He worshiped the Almighty God as the One who was higher, more glorious and more powerful than anyone else.

But one day Lucifer, for the very first time, had a bad thought–a very bad thought. He no longer wanted to think how wonderful God is. But he began to think of himself and how beautiful he was. To himself he said something that was very wrong: "I want to be like God who is the highest of all. I want to have His majesty and power." Lucifer wanted to take the place of Almighty God. Imagine that! He was no longer satisfied simply to rule over other angels. He wanted the angels to worship him as they worshiped God.

As Lucifer thought he began to plan: "I will go into the highest Heaven. I will have my throne above the stars of God. I will rule above the clouds." His desire for power went on and on. He wanted to be as high as God. The desire of Lucifer was sin–the very first sin.

God, who is holy, could not permit sin–not even the sin of pride–in Heaven. So Lucifer was punished by having his high position taken from him. No longer was he called Lucifer (meaning *Daystar*). His name was changed to Satan (*the devil*).

How Satan hated God! Never again would he obey and serve God. Now he would rule for himself. He hated all the good plans of God, and he decided to spoil those plans with the power that God had let him keep. Satan made his own plans–plans to do evil work against God.

2. ADAM AND EVE, CONTROLLED BY SATAN, SIN
Genesis 3:1-24

Show Illustration #14

When God made the first man and woman, Satan wanted to be worshiped by them, just as he had wanted the angels to worship him. Everything was beautiful and perfect in the Garden of Eden. There were no wild animals. All were tame and friendly. Even the serpents were harmless–and doubtless pretty. There was nothing of which to be afraid in that beautiful place. So Satan, in the form of a serpent, went to Eve. There, in that lovely garden, Satan tempted Eve to disobey God. She listened to him and–would you believe it?–she decided to disobey God! And that was sin. Adam sinned, too. And ever since that day everyone born into this world (except the Lord Jesus Christ) has been a sinner–all because of Satan, the enemy of God.

3. CHRIST DIES FOR SINNERS
Genesis 3:15

But God did not let Satan have his own way. He upset Satan's plans. God promised that He would send a Deliverer–a Saviour–who would one day destroy Satan. (See Genesis 3:15.)

Satan was very angry and tried to keep the promise of God from coming true. He knew that the Deliverer whom God had promised would come from the nation Israel. So Satan tried again and again to destroy the Israelites. He hated God's chosen people. But God would not let His people be completely destroyed.

No matter how hard Satan tried, he could not change the plan of God. He could not keep the Deliverer from coming to earth as God had promised. Jesus was the Deliverer, and one night He was born in Bethlehem. But Satan had not given up. Through King Herod, he tried to destroy the baby Jesus. Herod commanded his soldiers to kill all the little boys in Bethlehem, two years old and under. But God protected Jesus by having Mary and Joseph take Him far away from Bethlehem (to Egypt).

Satan tried to get the Lord Jesus to sin. If he could get Jesus to disobey God the Father, Jesus would no longer be perfect. If He was not perfect, He would not be able to save people from their sins. But God is stronger than Satan. And, since Christ Jesus is God the Son, He did not sin.

Did Satan stop fighting God? No! Another time he tried to get rid of Jesus by causing the people of Nazareth to try to push Jesus off a high cliff. But God the Father protected His Son. The people could not kill Jesus for it was not yet the time God had chosen for Him to die. God was proving that He had much more power than Satan and that His promises always come true.

Show Illustration #15

The Lord Jesus always did what God the Father wanted Him to do. He lived a perfect life on earth, and one day He gave His life as a perfect sacrifice on the cross. It looked as if Satan had finally won when Jesus died. But he was in for a great surprise!

4. SATAN DEFEATED
Revelation 20:10

Show Illustration #16

After three days the Lord Jesus was raised from the dead by the power of God. Jesus had overcome Satan by His death on the cross and His resurrection from the dead. He rose again and He lives today. He will always live. The day is coming when Satan will be punished for his sin and disobedience. He will be punished forever in the Lake of Fire, just as God has promised. (See Revelation 20:10.)

What is Satan doing today? Although we cannot see him, he is very busy. He is trying to keep people from receiving the Lord Jesus. (See 2 Corinthians 4:3, 4.) We are all sinners. We all have chosen to go our own way instead of God's way. (See Isaiah 53:6.) We cannot get loose from our sin. It is as if all of us were tied tightly with ropes. Our arms, our legs, every part of our body is tied. And because all of us are tightly tied, none can help the other. But there is One who is not tied. He never sinned! He, the sinless Son of God, is the only One who can free us from the sin that binds us. And when we truly believe that He is the Son of God; and when we believe that He took the punishment for our sins when He died on the cross; and when we receive Him as Saviour, He forgives our sin. He sets us free! We become members of the family of God.

But even after we belong to the Lord God, Satan does not leave us alone. He tries to cause the children of God to do all kinds of wrong: lie, steal, cheat, hate, fight, be proud and disobey God in all kinds of ways. (See Acts 5:3; 1 Peter 5:8.)

We cannot fight Satan by ourselves. He is more powerful than you or I. How can we overcome him when he is stronger than we are? The Bible tells us to give ourselves to God and obey Him. Then with His help, as we stand up to the devil, he will run away from us. (See James 4:7.) But Satan will return again and again to try to trick us into doing wrong. He is a liar and the "father of lies" (John 8:44). If Satan does get you to do wrong, he goes to God and tells Him how awful you are. He wants to get you into all the trouble he can.

What should a child of God do if he sins? He should confess his sin to God right away. God will forgive those who are really sorry for what they have done. (See 1 John 1:9.)

It seems that more people today are listening to Satan than are listening to God. But someday everyone will bow before God and His Son, Jesus Christ. (See Romans 14:11; Philippians 2:9-11.) And Satan and all who have followed him–those who have never accepted the Lord Jesus Christ–will be punished forever in the Lake of Fire.

Are you on the side of God or on the side of Satan? Remember, those who are on the side of God are on the winning side! If you believe that Jesus Christ is the Son of God, if you believe He died and rose again for you, and if you want to receive Him as your Saviour today, please tell me so right after class. I would like to talk with you about it.

Teacher: Before using the lessons in the next volume, it would be well to make certain that your students have understood the lessons in this series. To be certain they have learned well, ask a few questions:

1. Before Adam and Eve lived in the Garden of Eden here on earth, where did Satan live? *(Heaven)*
2. When he lived in Heaven, what was he like? *(Beautiful)*
3. What high position did Satan have in Heaven? *(Son of the Morning, God's appointed)*
4. What did Satan do that made him lose his high position in Heaven? *(He desired to be over God.)*
5. Is Satan now a friend or an enemy of God? *(Enemy)*
6. Who is greater–Satan or God? *(God)*
7. Does Satan want people to sin against God? *(Yes!)*
8. What must we do to become members of the family of God? *(Believe that Jesus is the Son of God, that He died and rose again and receive Him as Saviour.)*
9. If (after receiving the Lord Jesus as our Saviour), we should sin, what must we do? *(Confess)*
10. What is the verse of Scripture that we have memorized while we have been studying these lessons? *(Ye are of God, little children, and have overcome them: because greater is He that is in you, than he that is in the world. 1 John 4:4)*

www.ingramcontent.com/pod-product-compliance
Lightning Source LLC
Chambersburg PA
CBHW060805090426
42736CB00002B/162